Investing and Trading

The Basic Investor's Library

Alternative Investments

Bonds, Preferred Stocks, and the Money Market

Careers in the Investment World

Growth Stocks

Investing and Trading

Investment Banking

Investments and the Law

Mutual Funds

Reading the Financial Pages

Stock Options

The Principles of Technical Analysis

Understanding A Company

Wall Street—How It Works

What Is a Share of Stock?

Chelsea House Publishers

Investing and Trading

JEFFREY B. LITTLE

Paul A. Samuelson
Senior Editorial Consultant

Rogers Middle/High
School Library
1 Eagle Drive
Rogers, TX 76569-4127

CHELSEA HOUSE PUBLISHERS   New York   New Haven   Philadelphia

Editor-in-Chief   Nancy Toff
Executive Editor   Remmel T. Nunn
Managing Editor   Karyn Gullen Browne
Copy Chief   Juliann Barbato
Picture Editor   Adrian G. Allen
Art Director   Giannella Garrett
Manufacturing Manager   Gerald Levine

Staff for   INVESTING AND TRADING
Senior Editor   Marjorie P. K. Weiser
Associate Editor   Andrea E. Reynolds
Assistant Editor   Karen Schimmel
Copyeditor   Ellen Scordato
Editorial Assistant   Tara P. Deal
Picture Researcher   Ilene Cherna Bellovin
Senior Designer   Laurie Jewell
Designer   Ghila Krajzman
Production Coordinator   Joseph Romano

Creative Director   Harold Steinberg

Contributing Editor   Robert W. Wrubel
Consulting Editor   Shawn Patrick Burke

Copyright © 1988 by Chelsea House Publishers, a divison of Main Line Book Co.
All rights reserved. Printed and bound in the United States of America.

First printing

1 3 5 7 9 8 6 4 2

Library of Congress Cataloging in Publication Data

Little, Jeffrey B.
  Investing and trading.
  (The Basic investor's library)
  Bibliography: p.
  Includes index.
  1. Stock-exchange—Juvenile literature.
2. Investments—Juvenile literature [1. Stock exchange. 2. Investments] I. Samuelson, Paul Anthony, 1915–
II. Title. III. Series
HG4553.L58   1988   332.6′78   87-23852
ISBN 1-55546-627-3

CONTENTS

Foreword: Learning the Tools of Investing
   by Paul A. Samuelson _____ 6
Financial Planning, Risks, and Rewards _____ 10
Choosing a Stockbroker _____ 15
Buying on Margin _____ 21
How Stocks Are Traded _____ 24
Dollar Cost Averaging _____ 27
Bear Market Strategies _____ 30
Taking Taxes into Account _____ 35
Arbitrage _____ 36
Becoming an Investor _____ 38
Further Reading _____ 44
Glossary _____ 45
Index _____ 46

Learning the Tools of Investing

PAUL A. SAMUELSON

When asked why the great financial house of Morgan had been so successful, J. Pierpont Morgan replied, "Do you suppose that's because we take money seriously?"

Managing our personal finances is a serious business, and something we all must learn to do. We begin life dependent on someone else's income and capital. But after we become independent, it is a remorseless fact of nature that we must not only support ourselves for the present but must also start saving money for retirement. The best theory of saving that economists have is built upon this model of *life-cycle saving*: You must provide in the long years of prime working life for what modern medicine has lengthened to, potentially, decades of retirement. This life-cycle model won a 1985 Nobel Prize for my MIT colleague Franco Modigliani, and it points up the need to learn the rudiments of personal finance.

Learning to acquire wealth, however, is only part of the story. We must also learn to avoid losing what we have acquired. There is an old saying that "life insurance is *sold*, not bought." The same goes for stocks and bonds. In each case, the broker is guaranteed a profit, whether or not the customer benefits from the transaction. Knowledge is the customer's only true ally in the world of finance. Some gullible victims have lost their lifetime savings to unscrupulous sales promoters. One chap buys the Brooklyn Bridge. Another believes a stranger who asserts that gold will quickly double in price, with no risk of a drop in value. Such "con" (confidence) rackets get written up in the newspapers and on the police blotters every day.

I am concerned, however, about something less dramatic than con artists; something that is not at all illegal, but that costs ordinary citizens a thousand times more than outright embezzlement or fraud. Consider two families, neighbors who could be found in any town. They started alike. Each worked equally hard, and had about the same income. But the Smiths have to make do with half of what the Joneses have in retirement income, for one simple reason: The Joneses followed prudent practice as savers and investors, while the Smiths tried to make a killing and constantly bought and sold stocks at high commissions.

The point is, it does matter to learn how financial markets work, and how you can participate in them to your best advantage. It is important to know the difference between *common* and *preferred* stocks, between *convertible* and *zero-coupon* bonds. It is not difficult to find out what *mutual funds* are, and to understand the difference between the successful Fund A, which charges no commission, or "load," and the equally successful Fund B, which does charge the buyer such a fee.

All investing involves risk. When I was a young assistant professor, I said primly to my great Harvard teacher, Joseph Schumpeter: "We should speculate only with money we can afford to lose." He gently corrected me: "Paul, there is no such money. Besides, a speculator is merely an investor who has lost." Did Schumpeter exaggerate? Of course he did, but in the good cause of establishing the basic point of financial management: Good past performance is no guarantee of the future.

That is why *diversification* is the golden rule. "Don't put all your eggs in one basket. And watch all those baskets!" However, diversification does not mean throwing random darts at the financial pages of the newspaper to choose the best stocks in which to invest. The most diversified strategy of all would be to invest in a portfolio containing all the stocks in the comprehensive Standard & Poor's 500 Stock Index. But rather than throw random darts at the financial pages to pick out a few stocks, why not throw a large bath towel at the newspaper instead? Buy a bit of everything in proportion to its value in the larger world: Buy more General Motors than Ford, because GM is the bigger company; buy General Electric as well as GM because the auto industry is just one of many industries. That is called being an *index investor*. Index investing makes sense because 70 out of 100 investors who try to do better than the Standard & Poor's 500, the sober record shows, do worse over a 30-year period.

Do not take my word for this. The second lesson in finance is to be skeptical of what writers and other experts say, and that includes being skeptical of professors of economics. So I wish readers *Bon voyage!* on their cruise to command the fundamentals of investing. On your mainship flag, replace the motto "Nothing ventured, nothing gained" with the Latin words *Caveat emptor*—Let the buyer beware.

7

Traders on the floor of the New York Stock Exchange.

Investing and Trading

Providing for an individual's or a family's financial needs over a long period of time is never as simple as earning money, putting it in the bank, and then withdrawing it as necessary to meet expenses. As careers progress and household makeup changes, income and expenses change, too. At each stage of life, different combinations of savings and investments are appropriate.

The noted financier Bernard M. Baruch once said, "There is no investment which does not involve some risk and is not something of a gamble." Experienced investors, familiar with the direct relationship between the risk level of a security and the reward it promises, would agree.

However, individuals' investment needs and objectives vary. Their expectations of risk and reward vary also, and so do their approaches to the stock market. This book will help new investors set realistic investment objectives and select a stockbroker. In addition, it explains such stock market details as buying on margin, bear market strategies, arbitrage, tax considerations for investors, investment clubs, and mutual funds.

FINANCIAL PLANNING, RISKS, AND REWARDS

Individuals, whatever their family status, must plan far ahead if they want to enjoy their income while remaining financially secure. Investments of one kind or another have a place in every financial plan. Investing should use only money that is *discretionary,* or not needed for current or short-term essential expenses. However, stock market investments are not the first choice of where to put any money that is not needed for immediate living expenses. Financial advisers universally recommend buying securities only after an individual or family has provided for three major contingencies:

1. Some money must be set aside to meet emergency needs. Experts recommend that an emergency fund equal to at least three months' expenses be kept accessible, perhaps in a bank savings account.
2. Property, health, and life insurance policies should be adequate for individual and/or family needs. Health and life insurance are often provided by an employer; homeowners and other insurance are generally purchased directly from an insurance company through a sales agent.
3. Money should be set aside for other obvious needs, such as to continue education or buy a home.

Setting Financial Goals

The first step in financial planning is to establish goals. Setting financial goals is nothing more than understanding what major expenditures are called for in the life-style you plan for yourself. For many people financial well-being generally means being able to take vacations, owning a home and a car, sending children to college, and being financially independent in retirement. These are long-term goals. Few people can pay for these as necessary out of current income. For this reason, people must put aside some money from current income to invest. The growth in value of their investments, they hope, will give them the money to finance their long-term goals. The money earmarked for investing is frequently referred to as *risk capital*, no matter how conservative the intended investment program might be, even if low-risk investments are selected.

After people decide on their financial goals, they can decide how to allocate their risk capital to meet those goals. Over time, however, investment goals change. People at early stages of their careers can tolerate more risk than older investors because they have more time to earn back what they might lose. For this reason young investors are often advised to choose stocks that may be risky but that offer greater potential for capital appreciation in the long run. On the other hand, older people looking ahead to retirement are more likely to be concerned with preserving the nest egg they have accumulated over the years. Usually advised to place safety and income above other investment considerations, they would perhaps hold more high-rated corporate and government bonds, which offer stability and steady income. A loss from a higher-risk investment could no longer be recouped out of earnings.

After retirement people are advised to invest for income and safety of principal, putting their capital into such securities as bonds and treasury bills. The fairly predictable life cycle of individuals and of families is an important guide to choice of investments.

Growth, Risk, and Reward

Investments are generally chosen to provide for income, capital appreciation, or safety, or some combination of these objectives.

Income refers to the amount of money the particular investment will provide on a regular and timely basis. Bonds that pay interest every three months generally offer the highest regular income. Common stocks provide income in the form of dividends, based on the earnings and profits of the company.

THREE APPROACHES TO INVESTING

Approach	Method	Risk/Reward Balance	Goal
Long-term	Hold stock 2 years or longer	Low risk, moderate reward	Accumulates dividends and expects stock to rise in value
Speculating	Depend on tips to seek out bargains	Substantial risk, uncertain reward	Turn a quick profit
Trading	Buy large blocks of stock, sell as soon as price rises slightly	High risk, but chance of high reward	Buy and sell frequently to take advantage of small gains in price

Capital appreciation refers to the growth of an initial investment amount, or principal. Common stocks, which can grow 30 to 40 percent in value in a year's time, have always offered the highest rates of capital appreciation. The gain is realized only when a stock is sold at a higher price than that which the investor paid for it. Common stocks may also produce income, in the form of dividends. There is great variation among individual stock issues in regard to growth and income. The price of growth stocks may rise rapidly whereas the more conservative "blue-chip" stocks often grow more slowly but pay dividends consistently. Of course, stocks can drop in value, too, and dividend payments may come to a halt. Bonds offer little capital appreciation potential, but do produce significant income, in the form of interest paid regularly to investors.

Safety is always a concern for investors. Investments vary widely in the safety they provide. There is a fairly constant relationship between risk and reward known as the *risk/reward ratio*. It is expressed in what is perhaps the most basic of all Wall Street concepts: The greater the expected return, the greater the investment risk.

This relationship arises out of a basic fact of a free securities market. Every investment carries some risk. All investors face the risk of losing some or all of the money originally invested. A security will not attract investors unless it promises a level of return high enough to justify an investor's risk in buying it.

FINANCIAL PLANNING

Several thorough studies of historic rates of investment returns have shown clear evidence of the risk/reward ratio. The general rule is that the less safe an investment, the higher its potential return to the investor. For example, a savings account in a bank is about as safe an investment as possible. The money will be there, earning interest periodically, albeit at a relatively low rate. There is no risk but no potential growth in value either. Bonds pay more interest, but are somewhat less safe than savings accounts. The corporation or government agency that issued the bonds may be unable to pay the interest on schedule if it experiences a downturn in its income. Some bond issues are more reliable than others, and bonds are identified by a rating of their risk level, from AAA ("triple A") for the safest to C for the most risky. The least safe type of investment, but the one with the greatest potential for growth, is common stock. There is no guarantee that a stock will not decline in value. The trade-off for the higher risk assumed by an investor in common stocks is a historic average return substantially higher than that of corporate bonds or treasury bills.

Although each investment category has its own risk/reward pattern, there are exceptions. For example, many low-quality (that is, somewhat risky) bonds provide a better return than a typical high-quality stock.

The risk/reward balance can change from one month to the next as investors respond to changes in interest rates, inflation, or other factors. For example, given an inflation rate of 5.5 percent and U.S. treasury bills paying 4.5 percent, savings accounts paying 5.0 percent, and corporate bonds paying 7.5 percent, one might conclude that a share of common stock, the most risky investment possibility, should provide a return of at least 10 percent to be competitive for the investor's dollar.

Selection and Timing

To be successful on Wall Street an investor must find a satisfactory combination of two key variables, selection and timing. As

A Woolworth store in Madison, Wisconsin, 1928.

a general rule investment selection and timing have an inverse relationship. When an investment is to be held for a long period of time, selection is the more important factor. For example, an investor who bought the common stock of F. W. Woolworth Co., the "5 and 10" retail chain, for $22 in early 1985 may have been somewhat bothered when it dropped slightly two months later. But after holding Woolworth for only one year, the investor saw the stock rise to $38, and after two and a half years, in July 1987, it reached about $55 per share. Timing is most important with short-term investments, which the beginner should avoid. A trader, who buys and sells a stock within a few months, would always be concerned with timing.

Estimating Total Return

A good way to compare the potential gain of several possible investment vehicles is to estimate the *total return* of each one. This is the increase in value over the expected life of the investment, calculated as a percent of current value or price. The table shows the percent return that can be expected for 5 investment choices: 4 percent return of a U.S. treasury bill, 5 percent from a bank savings account, 9 percent from a corporate bond, and 12 percent from each of 2 common stocks.

**COMPARISON OF TOTAL EXPECTED RETURN
OF FIVE HYPOTHETICAL INVESTMENTS**

Investment Choice	Possible Capital Appreciation	Dividend or Interest Yield	Total Return
Growth Stock X	10%	2%	12% *(earnings per share growth + dividend yield)*
Income Stock Y	7%	5%	12% *(earnings per share growth + dividend yield)*
Corporate Bond Z	2%	7%	9%* *(bond discount to maturity + interest yield)*
Savings Account	0	5%	5%
Treasury Bill	4%	0	4%

* *Also called "yield to maturity."*

The estimated total return on these stocks may be the same, but its source is different. Stock X is from a company that is growing; stock Y is from a company that has not missed paying dividends in more than 10 years. Growth stock X probably represents higher initial market risk and greater reward over time than the slower-growing but higher-yielding stock Y. There might be less risk at first in obtaining 12 percent from the income stock, but a patient investor would probably see a greater total return from higher future earnings of the growth stock.

CHOOSING A STOCKBROKER

In order to buy stock, it is necessary to have a stockbroker. Investors cannot buy stock directly from the company that issues the stock, but must do so from an account executive (AE), or registered representative, at a brokerage firm. A stockbroker may be recommended by family, friends, or business associates. Expertise, personality, and reputation are all important qualifications. It is best if the investor can get referrals to two or three people. Personal conversations with each candidate will help the investor select the person who seems most suitable.

In evaluating an interview the investor should consider the stockbroker's personality and investment philosophy. Other factors to consider are the quality of the firm's research, any other services the firm may provide, and the commission rates the investor is able to negotiate. Recommendations from other clients of the brokerage firms being considered are useful for comparing services and efficiency.

A qualified stockbroker will be employed by a reputable brokerage firm, preferably one that is a member of the New York Stock Exchange (NYSE). A stockbroker for a member firm will most likely have completed an extensive training course and passed a comprehensive test prepared by the NYSE and the National Association of Securities Dealers before being approved by the Securities and Exchange Commission (SEC).

It is not necessary to visit a brokerage office to open an account. Stockbrokers spend a great deal of time on the telephone with their clients.

Account executives are required to follow a strict code of ethics and obey a number of rules. They are, for example, forbidden to guarantee any client against a loss, cannot share in the profits or losses of a client's account, and may not rebate any of their compensation to clients.

After an investor selects a stockbroker, there should be a conference to review the client's investment objectives. The topics discussed should include the investor's age and family circumstances, income, amount of personal debt and interest payments, if any, adequacy of savings and insurance, and any anticipated changes in the investor's situation, such as receiving an inheritance or making a job change.

The brokerage firm charges a commission each time stock is bought and sold. The stockbroker, as an employee of the firm, will receive a portion of that fee. At one time commissions were set by the NYSE, but an SEC ruling made this fee negotiable since May 1975. The commission on a $3,000 transaction, for example the purchase or sale of 100 shares of a $30 stock, might come to about $58 (about 1.9 percent). Depending on the firm's policy, the stockbroker's share might be $15 to $20. A stockbroker's income obviously increases if stock is bought and sold more frequently. Frequent trading, however, might not be in the client's best interest. A broker who urges frequent trades is said to be "churning." This practice is contrary to SEC regulations and can result in severe penalties to the broker and the firm. Most stockbrokers avoid such questionable behavior; they know it is to their advantage to help each client become a successful investor.

How to Work with a Stockbroker

Stockbrokers should not be judged by the short-term ups and downs of the stock they recommend. They can neither control stock prices nor consistently predict them. They should be judged primarily by the quality of service they provide.

Clients should heed their AEs' advice. They should use stockbrokers as a valuable information source and feel free to ask for research reports and other investment data that can help them make investment decisions. The ultimate decision to buy or sell, however, rests entirely with the client. Investors should be explicit when placing an order or giving instructions, to avoid misunderstandings.

Investors should accumulate their own research sources. Stock guides, investment handbooks, annual reports, and other research material kept in home files will ease the job of searching for background information.

Discount Brokers

Most investors want and need the recommendations and individual stockbroker relationships provided by full-service brokerage firms. However, discount brokerages should be considered by investors who expect to make their own decisions.

Discount firms offer low commissions and "no-frills" services and may be good choices for investors who anticipate trading a great deal and would face high commission costs. There is usually a minimum transaction charge of $20 to $30. Some discount brokers require a modest deposit or a minimum annual commission. For an active investor trading 15 or 20 times or more each year the savings could be considerable.

After fixed commission rates were abolished in 1975 the number of discount brokers increased dramatically. Today, discount brokerage firms can be found in many major cities. A discount firm that is being considered should be investigated in the same way as a full-service brokerage.

Opening an Account

Opening a brokerage account is similar in many ways to opening a charge account at a local store or a checking account with a bank. The individual must demonstrate a satisfactory credit rating; there are certain levels of financial requirements; the account can be held by a single individual or jointly owned; and the client receives a monthly statement. The typical stock brokerage office contains a "gallery" area where clients can view stock prices on computer monitors. In addition, there is usually a collection of reference books, analysts' research reports, and other investment material available. It is usually not necessary to have an account with the brokerage firm to visit the office.

Types of Accounts

There are two basic types of brokerage accounts: *cash accounts* and *margin accounts*. Many brokerage firms offer both. With a cash account, which is by far the most popular, every transaction is concluded on or before the settlement date, and cash changes hands directly between client and brokerage. If stock has been purchased, the client pays for it in full, the client's broker pays the seller's broker, and the shares are credited to the buyer's account, all within five business days.

With a margin account, the client is able to borrow from the broker part of the purchase price of securities. The NYSE requires a minimum of $2,000 to open a margin account. As with a cash account, all transactions must be concluded by the settlement date, but a customer buying "on margin" does not have to pay in full. The brokerage extends credit based on the client's cash balance and/or already owned securities in the account. In exchange for this credit, the client at some point pays interest to the broker.

Trading

The day on which a share of stock is bought or sold is known as the *trade date*. The client must deposit the required cash and/or securities into his or her account on or before the fifth business day after the trade date. This deadline is known as the *settlement date*. Bond trades are settled the next day. Business days do not include Saturdays, Sundays, or holidays.

When investors give buy orders to their stockbrokers, they can also give instructions for any of the following procedures to be followed after the stock is purchased:
1. The stock can be "transferred and shipped." Transfer refers to the legal change of ownership of a stock certificate. It is then sent (shipped) to the owner. This process is usually handled by a transfer agent, such as a bank, and normally takes about two weeks. The transfer agent keeps records of the names and addresses of registered shareholders and the number of shares each owns. The transfer agent also sees that the transfer process is carried out accurately, and that new stock certificates are issued in the name of the new owner. After receiving a stock certificate, the stockholder must then find a safe place to keep it. Replacing lost or destroyed stock certificates is tedious and time-consuming.
2. The stock can be "transferred and held." After the new owner's name is transferred and a new certificate made out, the certificate is kept in the brokerage firm's vault. Subsequently, when the stock is sold, the owner must sign a "stock power" authorizing its transfer to the new owner.
3. The stock can be "held in street name." This means that it is safely held by the brokerage in the broker's name for the client's convenience. Dividends, which are sent directly to the stockholder when the stock has been transferred, are in this case credited to the stockholder's account at the brokerage, or forwarded monthly, as the client directs. Corporate reports and proxy statements are forwarded to the client.

The monthly statement from a brokerage is similar to a bank statement in appearance. It shows a beginning balance, all transactions made during the period, a final cash balance, and stock holdings at the end of the period.

Buying Stock for Minors

Brokerages generally will not accept accounts for minors, who can legally choose to cancel a contract. For this reason, giving

People who work in the operations departments at brokerages handle the extensive paperwork and computerized record keeping of the firm's clients.

securities to minors and having shares registered in minors' names presented problems until 1956 when states began passing the Uniform Gifts to Minors Acts as advocated by the investment industry. Under these laws, minors can own securities received as gifts, with an adult serving as "custodian." Usually the adult is the parent or another close relative, and the donor or gift giver. This has been a way for many families to plan for the costs of college and professional education for their children. The adult is supposed to manage these custodial accounts for the benefit of the minor. The specific provisions of these laws differ among the states. Stock ownership for minors is also affected by current tax laws. It is advisable to consult an accountant or financial planner before opening a custodial account.

Getting Professional Advice

A professional investment adviser can be extremely useful for those clients with a substantial amount of money to invest (at least $100,000) who are not interested in mutual funds, or have neither the time nor the inclination to supervise their own portfolios. Advisers' fees vary but typically start at 1 or 1.5 percent annually on portfolios up to about $200,000. As the amount invested increases, the percentage declines. The investor must still pay brokerage commission fees and may designate a stockbroker or let the adviser make the choice of a broker.

Trust departments of many banks also offer advisory and other services. There is usually a minimum account balance for an investor to make use of these services, which typically include both portfolio management and custodial functions, such as safekeeping of securities, dividend or interest collection and disbursements, and other accounting tasks.

Investors who want no involvement with their own affairs will open a *discretionary* account with an adviser or portfolio manager. This kind of account, in which the adviser has complete control of the investor's affairs, is often chosen by investors who hold elected office and might have conflicts of interest if they managed their own investments. Most investors, though, will prefer to open *nondiscretionary* accounts, which keep the investor involved and make it possible to learn a great deal about the investment process.

BUYING ON MARGIN

Using a *margin account* can be complex, but it gives the serious investor not only the advantage of buying securities on credit but also flexibility.
A margin account makes it possible to pay only a part of (perhaps half) the total amount of cash needed to buy the stocks. A brokerage house in effect lends the investor the remaining amount needed to make the purchase. Buying on margin is like taking out any other kind of loan. Interest must be paid to the brokerage, in addition to the commission due on the full price of the stocks.

Buying on margin magnifies the effect of an increase in a stock's price. On the other hand, if the stock declines in price, the magnifying effect will work in the opposite direction. Margin accounts are used largely by speculators, investors who are willing to take large risks in hope of making large gains.

Opening a Margin Account

When opening a margin account, investors must present information to verify their credit, if they do not have other accounts with the brokerage. They are asked to sign an agreement that any stock bought on margin will be held by the brokerage firm as *collateral*, becoming the property of the brokerage if the loan is not repaid on schedule. They must also sign a stock-loan consent form, which permits the brokerage to pledge or lend securities carried for the account.

Professional financial consultants provide investors with information about the range of investment possibilities that meet their respective needs.

Margin accounts are subject to various regulations. The Federal Reserve Board (the Fed) is the agency that regulates the use of credit for securities purchases. Regulation T of the Fed states the limit of margin loans, expressed as a percent of the total cost of the stock being bought. This amount, which may change over time, is now 50 percent. This means that an investor must put up cash equal to half of the total cost of the securities being purchased. The initial margin requirement for stocks, which has been raised 12 times and lowered 10 times since 1934, has been as low as 40 percent (1937) and as high as 100 percent (1946).

Other restrictions on margin accounts are set by the NYSE, including an *initial minimum requirement* or the least amount of money with which an investor can open a margin account. There is currently a $2,000 minimum required to open an account. Another NYSE requirement is the *maintenance margin*, the amount below which a margin account may not drop after the initial purchase. This is currently 25 percent. However, some brokerage firms establish their own maintenance margins, which may be slightly higher, perhaps 30 percent. A customer whose account balance falls below the maintenance margin will receive a *margin call* from the broker, requesting the deposit of additional funds to bring the account back to the required level.

Margin requirements often vary for different types of securities. There are many details investors should learn before using a margin account. A brokerage firm can provide specific information.

How a Margin Account Works

If an investor deposited $6,000 cash in a margin account and decided to purchase stock with a current market value of $9,000, a brokerage would be lending an investor $3,000. This amount, known as the *debit balance*, would be less than the 50 percent margin requirement. A record of this transaction would look like this:

Current Market Value	$9,000
Debit Balance	3,000
Current Equity	$6,000
Required Margin (50% x $9,000)	4,500
Excess Margin	$1,500

The actual amount paid by the investor is known as *current equity*. The required margin is $4,500, 50 percent of the current market value. In this case, the investor has paid into the account $1,500 more than he has to. This amount, known as *excess margin*, can be withdrawn or invested. If it is invested through the margin account, it will have a "buying power" of $3,000. That is, the investor can use it to buy $3,000 worth of additional stock on margin.

Debit balance is money loaned to the investor by the brokerage firm and on which the brokerage firm charges interest. This is the carrying cost of the securities. When interest rates charged by commercial banks are high, the carrying cost of margined securities can be extremely high, too.

The most important reason investors use margin is to gain *leverage*. Leverage refers to the ability of a margin account to magnify the gains or the losses of an investment. For example, if the market value of the $9,000 portfolio described on page 22 rises $2,000, or 22 percent, to $11,000, the investor's equity increases 33 percent and buying power becomes 67 percent greater.

Current Market Value	$11,000
Debit Balance	3,000
Current Equity	$ 8,000
Required Margin (50% x $11,000)	5,500
Excess Margin ($5,500 buying power)	$ 2,500

But if instead of rising the value of the portfolio drops $2,000, or 22 percent to $7,000, the results would be quite different. In this case, equity *decreases* 33 percent and buying power declines 67 percent.

Stockbrokers, who must be aware of market trends that affect their clients' investments, keep track of the latest developments with the aid of computers and telephones.

Current Market Value	$7,000
Debit Balance	3,000
Current Equity	$4,000
Required Margin (50% x $7,000)	3,500
Excess Margin ($1,000 buying power)	$ 500

At most brokerage firms margin accounts are handled by a margin department. Computers are used to review every account daily. This review, for example, checks to see whether a margin customer's equity has fallen below the current federal initial margin or the NYSE or brokerage house maintenance requirements. An account that is below the initial margin requirement is considered "restricted," which means that the investor has no additional buying power and cannot withdraw more than 30 percent of any sale proceeds. The remaining 70 percent would be retained to reduce the debit balance. An account that falls below the maintenance requirement is subject to a margin call, a request that the investor make a payment into the account.

HOW STOCKS ARE TRADED

Your stockbroker, or AE, acts as an agent on your behalf and does not actually buy or sell the stocks you choose. The broker's firm will be a member of various stock exchanges, or have a working relationship with a member firm. When you give an order to your broker, it is sent to the trading department of the broker's firm, and from there to the firm's representative, known as a *floor broker*, at the appropriate stock exchange. There are nine exchanges in the United States and many more in other countries. In addition, stocks are traded widely in the over-the-counter (OTC) market.

After floor brokers receive an order, they go to the *trading post* where that particular stock is bought and sold. At each trading post there is a *specialist* who handles trade in a number of stocks. At the trading post, buy orders are matched to sell orders, and the specialist keeps track of all transactions. If a buy or sell order cannot be carried out immediately, it is recorded in the *specialist's book* and transacted when possible. After a trade takes place, the details of price and numbers of shares are recorded immediately and the information is sent by computer network to brokers throughout the country.

Shares are sold by the *lot*. A *round lot* consists of 100 shares, and most stocks are sold in round lots. An *odd lot* consists of fewer than 100 shares.

Placing an Order with a Broker

When investors desire to buy or sell stock, they give instructions, or orders, to a broker. Each order to buy or sell may be given for a single specified period of time such as a trading day, week, or month. An *open order*, also called a *good 'til canceled (GTC)* order, stands until it is canceled by the investor. A stockholder can give any of several types of orders to a broker. The type of order chosen reflects the investor's strategies and financial situation at a given time.

The Market Order The *market order* to buy or sell is the most widely used type. It is simply an instruction to the stockbroker to buy or sell stock for the investor at the best price obtainable when the order reaches the trading post or trading desk. Normally, a market order is executed at a price reasonably close to the most recent quote obtained before the order was entered. If the stock is volatile, however, with frequent shifts in price, the final price could be better or worse than

expected. It normally takes only a few minutes to complete a market order transaction. In most cases, confirmation of the transaction is mailed to the investor within 24 hours.

The Limit Order The *limit order* is an instruction to buy or sell a stated amount of stock at a specific price or better (that is, lower for buying or higher for selling). When the target price requested by the investor is not within the current market quote, it is said to be "away from the market." A price that is away from the market will be entered on the specialist's book after any similar orders received earlier. If there are "shares ahead of you," your limit order may not be executed immediately, or may not be transacted at all at that price. As the quoted price of a stock begins to approach the target price of the limit orders entered in the book, the specialist executes the transactions in the order in which they are listed. For the OTC market where there is no specialist, limit orders are held in the brokerage firm's inventory until the stock reaches the target price.

The Stop Order The *stop order* (at one time known as a stop-loss order) can protect a profit or prevent further loss if a stock's price begins to move in the wrong direction. This idea is based on the ageless Wall Street advice: "Let your profits run; cut your losses short." The stop order becomes a market order when the stock trades at or through a certain price, known as the "stop price."

For example, you buy 100 shares of the stock of XYZ Company at a price of $10 a share, and in a year the price of the stock goes up to $20. You studied the company and decided that when the stock reached $20 there was a good chance its price would start to decline, so you gave your broker a stop order at $18. If the stock continues to go up in value, you will continue to hold on to the stock. However, if it declines from $20 to $18, as you think is possible, your broker must try to sell it at or as close as possible to the price of $18. This way you cut your potential losses and lock in a gain.

There is, however, no guarantee that your order will be executed at the exact price you have requested. Suppose the stock of XYZ Company has dropped below $18 when your order actually reaches the trading floor. You will get a confirmation that your stock was sold at 17½. In general, a stop price should not be too close to the current market price, because many stocks normally fluctuate 14 percent or more in a brief period of time. Short-term investors who trade in and out of the market are more likely than long-term investors to use the stop order as a trading tool.

The Stop Limit Order The *stop limit order* combines features of the stop order and limit order. A stop limit order to buy means that, as soon as a trade occurs at the stop price or higher, the order becomes a limit order to buy. A stop limit order to sell means that, as soon as a trade occurs at the stop price or lower, the order becomes a limit order to sell.

DOLLAR COST AVERAGING

There are no magic formulas to stock market investing, but one widely used and frequently successful approach is *dollar cost averaging*. Dollar cost averaging is based on the historic fact that stock prices tend to rise over a long period of time. This strategy for long-term gain involves purchasing the same dollar amount of a stock at regular intervals regardless of price per share. More shares can be bought when the per-share price is low. After several years, the shares bought at lower prices make up for or average out the cost of shares bought at higher prices.

Successful use of dollar cost averaging requires that an investor do the following:
- Invest for a period of at least several years.
- Plan to invest at regular intervals—two, three, or four times a year—no matter what the price of the stock chosen.
- Choose a high-quality stock that, preferably, pays a dividend.
- Select a company that has favorable growth prospects that could lead to a rising stock price over the long term.
- Invest a minimum of $1,000 per year (commission costs are quite high otherwise).
- Be willing to continue the program relentlessly—barring any substantial change in the company's long-term outlook.

Dollar cost averaging is ideal for investors who want to participate in the stock market but are afraid of buying a stock at too high a price. This strategy eliminates much of the risk of buying stocks whose price may fluctuate over time. Meanwhile, dividends accumulate. The effect of dollar cost averaging is to limit your buying when a stock is expensive and expand your buying power when the stock is cheap.

STOCK PERFORMANCE OF THE MIGHTY WIDGET COMPANY

Year	Annual Price Range High Low	Shares Bought	Shares Owned at Year End	Average Price per Share	Annual Dividend (estimated)
1	$62⅝–$46¾	36	36	$55½	$25
2	54⅜–41⅝	42	78	51¼	68
3	56–42⅞	41	119	50⅜	118
4	49⅜–31⅜	54	173	46⅛	175
5	46⅝–24	58	231	43¼	242
6	38⅛–25⅞	59	290	41⅜	313
7	53⅝–31⅞	49	339	41¼	399
8	52⅝–25⅞	52	391	40⅞	489
9	50¼–27⅛	49	440	40⅞	557
10	61¼–38½	37	477	41⅞	628

The table above shows the results of a 10-year dollar cost averaging investment program for the hypothetical Mighty Widget Company. Our investor decided to put $500 every three months, or $2,000 a year, into Widget stock. After 10 years the total investment was $20,000, of which about $800 went to the broker in commissions. Overall, Mighty Widget's performance was disappointing in this period. Stock prices in the first year varied from a low of $46.75 to a high of $62.53, and in year 10 traded in about the same range ($38.50 to $61.25). But our investor saw holdings accumulate most quickly when the stock price was lowest, in years 5 and 6.

Widget's earnings were modest, staying at about $3 to $4 per share per year for the entire period, as our investor found in reading the company's annual report. This resulted in dividends that increased just slightly, from $1.03 to $1.37 per share over the 10 years. (Fractional dividends were paid on shares held less than a year.) Dividends obviously become more important as time passes and total holdings increase.

Over the entire period, dollar cost averaging successfully reduced the average price paid per share to about $42. Income was good, with dividends in year 10 totaling about 12 percent of the total investment. This case illustrates how dollar cost averaging can help a long-term investor who selects a stock that is relatively stable in price and earnings. There were, of course, many possible investments in the same period that would have produced better—and worse—results than Mighty Widget.

BEAR MARKET STRATEGIES

Stock prices have always gone up over the very long term. A period in which stock prices are going up steadily is known as a *bull market*. Most investors are very sure of what to do in a bull market: Buy the stocks that seem most likely to increase in price and sell them at

A trading specialist on the floor of the New York Stock Exchange reacts to falling stock prices on October 19, 1987. That day, the Dow Jones Industrial Average dropped an unprecedented 508 points.

A stockbroker at Drexel Burnham Lambert takes calls from customers trying frantically to sell their securities during the October 1987 stock market crash.

the top of the market, before they decline. But the stock market does not advance in a straight line. There are periods, sometimes several years long, in which stock prices generally decline. These are known as *bear markets*.

Since World War I there have been more than 10 major bear markets in which stocks declined dramatically. In the stock market crash of 1929–32, in 1973–74, and in 1987, the market as a whole dropped significantly, and the values of hundreds of stocks were reduced by 30 percent or more. Moreover, it is a general rule that prices often go down faster than they go up. While most investors try to preserve capital in a bear market, the risk-oriented investor may see market weakness as an opportunity to make a substantial profit. There are several strategies for making money in a bear market.

Buying Contramarket Stocks When most prices on the stock market are advancing, the price of a contramarket stock will be going down. When most prices on the stock market are declining, the price of a contramarket stock will be going up. A contramarket stock is one whose price is moving in the opposite direction from that of most stocks at a given time. An astute in-

BEAR MARKET
STRATEGIES

31

A broker phones an option client to discuss possible moves, based on late market price information.

vestor who can identify a contramarket stock and invest in it during a bear market will not see the stock's value decline. A contramarket stock is especially noticeable as it continues to make steady gains in a bear market when everything else is dropping. An entire industry may go against the market for one reason or another. Each bear market is different. Industry groups that outperformed the market in the last few decades included oil and gas in 1946; pharmaceuticals, food, and tobacco in 1957; gold briefly in 1962; and coal and automobile replacement parts in 1969–70. The worst bear market since the 1930s occurred in 1973–74 when gold, sugar, steel, and fertilizer stocks were in favor.

After a bear market ends, contramarket stocks do not follow a definite pattern. Sometimes they continue rising, but sometimes they turn down almost at once. Investors should always study a company before buying its stock. It is inadvisable to buy astock simply because it is going up when other stocks are declining.

Buying Put Options   An *option* is the right, but not the obligation, to buy or sell a security at a certain time for a given price. Investors buy options but do not have to exercise them if they feel the market is unfavorable. Options can give active investors some additional flexibility in taking advantage of the ups and downs of the market.

A *put option* is a contract to sell (put) 100 shares at a definite price within a specified time limit. The investor who buys a put option has purchased a contractual right to "put" the stock to someone else. An investor in put options expects the stock price to be going down in the short term and will make a profit by selling before the stock price declines. There are two primary reasons for buying a put option in a bear market. The first is to make a quick gain by selling the put just before the stock's price declines. Secondly, if the investor buys a put option in addition to owning a particular stock, the put serves as a defensive hedge against a decline in the stock's value. If the stock price declines, the investor will lose money on the stock but make money on the put. The effect is to cancel out any loss. Of course, if the stock rises in price the opposite will occur: The investor will probably decide not to exercise the put, thus losing the money paid for the put in the first place, but will be able to pocket a gain on the stock itself, thus canceling the loss on the put.

Writing Naked Call Options A *call option* is a contract to buy (call) 100 shares at a definite price within a specified time limit. The investor who buys a call option has purchased a contractual right to "call" the stock from someone else. An investor who buys a call expects the stock price to rise in the short term. An investor who expects the price to decline may sell or "write" a call. An investor who owns 100 shares of a stock and believes its price might be going down can write a call option against those shares and sell the option to someone who believes the stock price will be going up. The investor gains by selling the option, canceling out a loss on the stock itself.

An option against stock that an investor owns is said to be "covered." It is also possible to write options against stock that an investor does not own. These are known as *naked options*. The writer of a naked call option is betting that the stock price is about to decline, so that the stock can be bought to cover the option at a lower price. Writing options is risky at best, and much can be lost. An investor who writes naked calls is a speculator willing to bet the stock price will not go up within the time limit of the contract.

Short Selling   The sale of securities that an investor does not own but borrows from a brokerage using a margin account is known as *short selling*. The investor is betting on actually buying the stock later at a lower price. Selling stock short is the best way to make money in a bear market, but it is appropriate only for investors who can afford the high risk.

In selling short, the normal sequence of purchase and sale is reversed. When stock is sold short, the brokerage firm either lends the stock to the customer or borrows it for the investor, who then sells it in the open market without actually owning it. Eventually, of course, the short seller will have to buy, or "cover," the same number of shares and return them to the lender. This is referred to as "short covering." If the price finally paid for the stock is lower than the price at which it was sold, the short seller will make a profit. However, if the stock price goes up, the short seller will have to pay more to cover the same number of shares and will suffer a loss. The investor will also be faced with a margin call, the need to add more money to the equity in the margin account, if the stock price goes up.

Suppose an investor decides that Baltimore Buggy Whip is likely to decline in value and sells short 100 shares at $70 a share. The investor needs to have $3,500 in his margin account to cover a possible purchase at the same price on 50 percent margin, and is soon able to deposit the proceeds, $7,000 (100 times $70) of the short sale as well. As expected, Baltimore Buggy Whip declines to $55 a share, and the short seller buys 100 shares to cover at a cost of $5,500, making a net profit on the transaction of $1,500. But suppose Baltimore Buggy Whip stock goes up to $85 a share. Now the short seller's equity would be reduced, since a maintenance margin of $4,250 would be required. However, there is still enough left in the margin account. But if the stock price really advances, the short seller may get a margin call and have to make an additional deposit to the account.

There is, moreover, an additional risk to short selling. The price of stock bought "long," that is, in the regular way, can never fall below zero. Thus a normal stock transaction can not involve a loss greater than the total investment. But the price of a stock sold short could, theoretically, rise without limit, and thus result in unlimited losses. To limit this potential loss, the short seller can use a stop order or purchase a call option as a hedge against the short position.

Even investors who are prepared to take risks should avoid short selling stocks likely to rise in price. They should, for example, avoid those that show gains in earnings or profits, those whose price has already declined considerably, and those that are merger candidates. For stocks in any of these categories, the risk of short selling would be too great.

TAKING TAXES INTO ACCOUNT

Active investors are constantly faced with tax decisions. Since passage of the Tax Reform Act of 1986, most investment income is not given preferential treatment, but is taxed at the same rate as ordinary income. Losses from investments up to $3,000 may be offset against ordinary income. This means that an investor who has sold stock for less than it cost can subtract the difference from income, and thus reduce the amount of income tax due. In some situations, it may be to an investor's advantage to take a loss in a given year.

President Ronald Reagan signs the 1986 Tax Reform Bill in a ceremony on the South Lawn of the White House, as various members of his administration and the Congress look on.

Investors should avoid waiting until late December to work out a tax strategy, but should evaluate their tax position throughout the year. Investors should also remember that to qualify for gains in a given year, stocks must be sold at least five business days (not including holidays) before year end. Tax laws are complex and change frequently. The tax situation for investors can be particularly intricate, and it is advisable to seek the help of an accountant. Most of the strategies suggested in this book will require expert guidance so that the investor will understand the tax implications of various investment choices.

ARBITRAGE

On Wall Street the term *arbitrage* used to refer to the simultaneous purchase and sale of two different but closely related securities (e.g., a convertibility of one security into the other) to take advantage of the difference in their prices. Before the stock exchanges were computerized, it was possible to find similar securities trading in different markets at slightly different

The chairman of Texas Air Corp., Frank Lorenzo, announces the merger of People Express and New York Air into its Continental Airlines subsidiary. Piled up around the podium are $5 million in $5 bills.

prices. Arbitragers would buy a security in one market and sell it in another market at a slightly higher price. The profits on each security were usually minute. But by investing large amounts of money, arbitragers could generate large profits on small discrepancies in price. Most of these traditional arbitrage opportunities have disappeared as investment markets have become more efficient.

However, one type of arbitrage, *merger* or *risk arbitrage*, has flourished on Wall Street in recent years. Merger arbitragers make money by investing heavily in the stocks of companies that are about to be acquired by another company. In a takeover attempt, the acquiring company offers to buy all the publicly owned shares of a target company. When the buyer has acquired a majority of the outstanding shares of the target company's stock, it can legally own the company. A trend toward takeovers gained considerable momentum in the 1980s. Many large American corporations and investors began buying the stocks of other large and small companies. They offered existing stockholders higher prices for their shares than the current market price. Investors eager to make a profit will naturally sell their stock to the acquiring company or investor. Usually, after the acquiring company makes its bid known to the public, the stock price of the target company jumps close to the offering price.

Merger arbitragers make money from these takeover situations in two ways. They try to identify companies that may be

ARBITRAGE

takeover targets before there is a public announcement. They stand to make enormous profits by selling the stock after an announcement sends the price up. "Arbs" may also invest in a takeover stock just after a merger is announced. Typically, the stock of a target company will continue to trade at a price just below that offered by the acquiring company until the merger agreement is actually signed, when the price reaches the offered level. This waiting period can last up to several months. This slight difference in price reflects the risk that the acquisition may be canceled at the last minute and the price of the stock would tumble back down to its previous level. The merger arbitrager accepts that risk and may continue to buy the stock until the very last day before the acquiring company actually purchases the remaining stock. The difference in price per share is small, but spread over the large number of shares owned by the "arb," the profit potential is substantial. Merger arbitrage is a risky investment practice with high stakes, requiring the investment of large sums of money to turn a profit. "Arbs" must be extremely knowledgeable about investments in general, and about possible takeover targets and industries in particular.

BECOMING AN INVESTOR

Many people would like to get started in investing but do not have large sums to commit or feel confident about choosing securities. They may want to consider learning more by joining an investment club or putting their money into a mutual fund and gaining the benefit of professional management.

Investment Clubs

Investment clubs typically consist of a small group, perhaps 10 to 15 people, that determines its investment objective, pools

Fidelity Investments has walk-in offices throughout the country where people may find out about and buy mutual funds. This is the customer service counter at Fidelity's 51st Street office in New York City.

members' money, chooses investments, and manages its own portfolio. Usually the club members meet monthly to review their collective investments. Each member makes a modest monthly contribution. The combined funds are often invested in growth stocks using a dollar cost averaging approach. Dividends and capital gains are generally reinvested.

There are about 7,000 investment clubs in the United States today. Many of them belong to the National Association of Investment Clubs (NAIC), a nonprofit organization that provides guidance and literature to its members. Individuals may join NAIC for a $10 annual fee; clubs pay $30 plus $7 per member.

Mutual Funds

In a sense, a mutual fund is like a much larger investment club whose portfolio is chosen and maintained by experienced professionals. Mutual funds are established by investment companies. Shares in the fund are sold to individual investors, and the fund invests in securities. In proportion to the number of fund shares they own, investors receive dividends and income realized when stock held by the fund is sold at a profit. In this way, each fund investor is part owner of a portfolio that is managed by professionals.

Investors can buy into a mutual fund with one payment, or they can pay a certain amount every month or every few months regularly, which offers the benefits of dollar cost aver-

At a Fidelity Investments walk-in office, a broker shows a client data for some of the many mutual funds managed by the company. Behind them is a kiosk containing literature about a variety of Fidelity's funds.

aging. Usually there are minimum amounts specified for single investment payments to a fund.

It is often assumed that the investment company is the "owner" of the fund. Actually, the shareholders own the fund and have the chance to vote on critical issues through mailed proxies just as they would if they owned common stock. Many investment companies manage more than one mutual fund, each with a different investment objective. Investors can often switch their money from one fund to another within the investment company "family" with just a quick phone call.

All mutual funds are closely regulated by the SEC. A prospectus that explains the fund, its investment objectives, and the risks involved must be made available to all potential investors. Investors also must be told of all charges. Most mutual funds are open-end funds. Such funds deal directly with investors and are always ready to sell more shares to or repurchase shares from investors at the current net asset value (NAV). Net asset value is the actual worth of a single share of the fund's stock. It is figured from the total value of all securities owned by the fund, minus all liabilities, with the difference divided by the number of shares outstanding. NAV is, thus, an accurate measure of the value of the holdings of an open-end fund at a given point in time. NAV is computed daily by investment companies, since the number of shares outstanding as well as the value of securities owned changes daily. To find out the net asset value of a fund, look in the financial section of any major newspaper.

From the investor's point of view, shares in an open-end fund can be bought or redeemed (sold back) at any time. As a result, money flows in or out of a mutual fund when investors subscribe to (join) the fund or redeem shares.

Closed-end funds, on the other hand, have a fixed number of shares outstanding. Investors can buy or sell these shares in the open market like any other stock. Because the market price rises or falls according to supply and demand, the price of a closed-end fund share may be set at a premium or, more likely, at a discount in relation to its net asset value. The price of a share in a closed-end fund, therefore, does not reflect the actual value of the securities held by the fund. For investors concerned about the net asset value of a fund's portfolio, an open-end fund is preferable to a closed-end fund. Some mutual funds have a sales charge, or "load," which is immediately deducted from an investor's payment before the investment is used to buy shares in the fund. The load is typically 8 percent of the investment. It serves as the commission for the sale of shares in the fund and also covers expenses of managing the fund. A no-load fund has no sales charge. Sales charges and other expenses are paid for out of gains in the fund's own holdings. All of the investor's payment goes to buy shares in the fund. Funds may charge additional fees when shares are redeemed. Investors should examine a fund's sales materials and prospectus carefully and question its representatives to learn the exact cost of investing in the fund. Because the initial higher cost of investing in a load fund reduces the amount of the investment that is actually working for the investor, no-load funds will overall give a better performance early on. They should be considered first, unless an investor has a strong reason to prefer a particular load fund management. It has been figured that a load fund portfolio must grow annually about 2 percent faster than a no-load fund portfolio to match the latter's performance over a five-year period.

Categories of Mutual Funds Investment companies usually offer several types of mutual funds in order to give potential investors a wide choice of investment objectives. Investors choose a particular fund because they are in agreement with its investment goals. There are five basic categories of mutual funds

1. *Common Stock Funds* invest almost entirely in equities (common stocks), although their objectives vary considerably. There are several types within this category. *Growth funds* seek capital appreciation by selecting companies that should grow more rapidly than the general economy. *Aggressive growth funds* buy shares in small or more speculative growth companies for maximum capital appreciation. *Growth and income funds* seek long-term capital appreciation with income. *Special purpose funds* attempt to satisfy certain investment interests, such as participation in gold or energy. *Index funds*, the newest type, buy stocks representative of a major stock market group in the hope of keeping pace with the generally long-term growth trend of the market.
2. *Income Funds* are portfolios consisting of bonds and common stocks as well as preferred stocks. Income fund managers try to obtain satisfactory interest and dividend income for the shareholders.
3. *Bond Funds* seek high income and preservation of capital by investing primarily in bonds and selecting the proper mix between short-term, intermediate-term, and long-term bond maturities. In recent years, tax-free *municipal bond funds* have been popular.
4. *Balanced Funds* buy both common stocks and bonds based on a popular belief that conditions unfavorable to common stocks are oftentimes favorable to bonds and vice versa.
5. *Money Market Funds* offer their shareholders a means of participating in the high-quality, short-term instruments of the money market, including certificates of deposit, treasury bills, and commercial paper.

Mutual funds are a good way to get started as an investor. The management of an investment company is as important a consideration when buying a mutual fund as the management of a corporation is when buying common stocks. The best way to identify a well-managed mutual fund is to look at its performance over the last 1, 5, and 10 years and compare it to other funds with similar objectives. Then consider what the fund's management is doing today: What is the fund's stated objective? What are its largest areas of investment? Do you know other investors who are satisfied with its performance for them? Many services, reports, and surveys analyzing mutual funds and their records can be found in the public library. With a few hours of research, an investor can construct a solid list of investment candidates.

FURTHER READING

Business Week, published weekly by McGraw-Hill, Inc., New York. Current financial and investment news can be found in the section on Markets and Investments.

Clairmont, George B., and Kiril Sokoloff. *Street-Smart Investing: A Price and Value Approach to Stock Market Profits.* New York: Random House, 1984. Evaluating risks, rewards, and stock market realities; how to choose stocks.

Engel, Louis, and Brendan Boyd. *How to Buy Stocks.* 7th rev. ed. Boston: Little, Brown, 1982. A classic; basic information about how stocks are bought and sold.

Klein, Robert J., and the editors of *Money* magazine. *The "Money" Book of Money: Your Personal Financial Planner.* Boston: Little, Brown, 1987. Practical, consumer-oriented guide to lifetime money management and planning.

Malkiel, Burton G. *A Random Walk Down Wall Street.* New York: Norton, 1981. Light style with solid content; historic events and trends in the investment industry; basic concepts of investing and a method for choosing common stocks.

Money, published monthly by Time Inc., New York. Features current information about financial planning, investing, and money management.

Quinn, Jane Bryant. *Everyone's Money Book.* New York: Dell, 1980. Clear explanations of everyday money management.

The Stock Market Magazine, published monthly by the Wall Street Publishing Institute, Inc., Yonkers, NY. The latest news for investors, from interviews with corporate managers, analysts, brokers, government officials, economists, and researchers.

Teweles, Richard J., and Edward S. Bradley. *The Stock Market.* New York: Wiley, 1982. A thorough explanation of the stock market, including trading-floor practices, client-broker relationships, and much more.

The Wall Street Journal, published weekdays by Dow Jones & Company, New York. The daily paper of the financial world covers business trends and the stock market.

And some resources: The Investment Company Institute (1800 M Street, NW, Suite 600, Washington, DC 20006) is the association of the mutual fund industry; publishes a fact book and brochures.

The National Association of Investment Clubs (1515 E. Eleven Mile Road, Royal Oak, MI 48068) offers materials about investing and publications.

GLOSSARY

account executive (AE), stockbroker An agent who acts as an intermediary between buyers and sellers of investments.

bear market A period of time during which stock prices decrease.

bond A certificate that represents a loan to a company (corporate bond) or government agency (municipal bond). The issuing company (the borrower) pays interest for the use of the money and must repay the entire amount of the bond at a specified time.

brokerage, brokerage firm, or *investment firm* An organization that facilitates the buying and selling of stocks and other types of investments. Account executives are employed by investment firms.

bull market A period of time during which stock prices increase.

capital appreciation The growth of an initial investment amount. Of possible investments, common stocks generally offer the best possibility of capital appreciation.

cash account A brokerage account in which cash is transferred directly between client and brokerage and in which the client pays in full when a purchase is executed.

collateral Valuable property used to secure a loan. If the borrower does not repay the loan, the collateral becomes the property of the lender.

contramarket stocks Stocks whose prices go against the movement of the market, rising when prices in general fall, and vice versa.

current equity The portion of the stock price that is paid for with money deposited by an investor in a margin account; does not include the money loaned by the broker.

custodial account A brokerage account owned on behalf of a minor (person below legal age) and managed by an adult, usually the minor's parent or guardian.

discount brokerage firm A company that buys and sells securities for clients at low commission costs, providing few services; attractive primarily to experienced and active investors.

discretionary account A brokerage account in which an adviser has complete control of the investor's affairs.

dividend A portion of a company's earnings that is distributed to its stockholders.

dollar cost averaging A strategy for long term gain that involves purchasing the same dollar amount of stock at regular intervals regardless of price.

floor trader A person who buys and sells equities directly on the floor of a stock exchange.

investment club A group of investors that determines collective investment objectives, pools members' money, and manages its own portfolio.

leverage The use of borrowed money, such as through a margin account, to magnify the potential gains (or losses) from an investment.

lot The measure of the number of stocks to be traded. A *round lot* contains 100 shares; an *odd lot* contains fewer than 100 shares.

maintenance margin The minimum amount of money that must remain in a margin account after the initial purchase.

margin call A request from a broker to a client to deposit additional money into a margin account whose balance has fallen below the maintenance margin.

margin account A brokerage account in which the client deposits a minimum amount to purchase securities, borrowing the remainder from the broker. In exchange for margin credit, the client pays interest to the broker.

market order An order from an investor to a broker to buy or sell a stock at the best price obtainable. A *limit order* directs the broker to buy or sell at a specific price. A *stop order* directs the broker to sell at or below a certain price, known as the stop price.

mutual fund An investment in which the money of many shareholders is combined in order to invest in a wide range of securities.

open order or good 'til canceled (GTC) order An order from an investor to a broker to buy or sell that remains in effect until canceled by the investor.

option The right, but not the obligation, to buy (call option) or sell (put option) a security at a certain time and for a certain price.

risk arbitrage or merger arbitrage The buying of the stock of a company that may soon be the target of a takeover bid in order to make a profit on the expected price increase.

risk capital Money intended for investment purposes.

risk/reward ratio An expression of the concept that the greater the expected return on an investment, the greater the investment risk.

Securities and Exchange Commission (SEC) A U.S. government agency established by Congress in 1934 to regulate the trading of stocks and bonds to protect investors.

settlement date The five-day deadline after the trade date by which the client must pay for purchased securities.

share of stock Any of the equal parts into which the entire value, or equity, of a company is divided. It represents part ownership in the company.

short selling The sale of securities not actually owned by the investor but borrowed from a brokerage using a margin account; the investor hopes to profit by selling the borrowed stock at a higher price. *Short covering* is the actual purchase of stock so it can be returned to the lending brokerage.

specialist The person at a trading post who records the prices of transactions in a limited number of specific stocks.

total return An estimate of the cumulative increase in value of an investment over its expected life; expressed as a percentage of current value.

trade date The day on which a share of stock is bought or sold.

trading post The area on a stock exchange floor where a particular stock is bought and sold.

INDEX

Advisers, financial, 14, 20–21
Annual report and corporate report, 17, 19, 29
Arbitrage, 9, 36–38

Bear market, 9
    trading strategies in, 30–35

Bonds, 11, 12, 13, 14, 42
Brokerage accounts, 17–18
Buying long, 35

Call option, 33, 35
Capital appreciation, 11–12, 42
Cash account, 18

Certificate of deposit, 42
Commissions and fees, 15, 16, 17, 20, 21, 28, 29, 41
Common stock, 11–15, 42–43
Contramarket stock, 31–32
Current equity, 23
Custodial account, 20

Debit balance, 22–24
Discretionary account, 20
Discretionary money or funds, 10
Dividends, 11–12, 15, 19–20, 28–30, 39
Dollar cost averaging, 28–30, 39–40

Earnings, 11, 29
Equity, 24, 42
Excess margin, 24

Interest, 13, 20, 23
Investment clubs, 9, 38–39
Investment goals or objectives, 10–11, 38
   of mutual funds, 42–43

Leverage, 23
Limit order, 26–27

Margin, margin account, 18, 21–24, 34
   restrictions, 22, 24
Market order, 25–26
Merger arbitrage, 37–38
Minors, buying stock for, 19–20
Mutual funds, 9, 20, 38–43

National Association of Investment Clubs (NAIC), 39
National Association of Securities Dealers (NASD), 15
Net asset value (NAV), 40–41
New York Stock Exchange (NYSE), 15, 22, 24
Nondiscretionary account, 21

Options, 32–35
Over-the-counter (OTC) market, 25–26

Profit, 11, 22, 25, 37–38. *See also* earnings
Prospectus, of mutual fund, 40, 41
Proxies and proxy statements, 19, 40
Put options, 32–33

Ratings, bonds, 13
Regulation T, 22
Risk, 9, 11, 15
Risk arbitrage, 37–38
Risk capital, 11
Risk/reward ratio, 12–13

Savings, 10, 11, 13
Securities, 18, 20–23, 36–38, 40–43
Securities and Exchange Commission (SEC), 15, 16, 40
Selection, 13–14
Settlement date, 18
Short covering, 35
Short selling, 34–35. *See also* options
Stocks. *See* common, contramarket, trading
Stockbroker and stockbrokerage, 9, 15–19, 21–25, 34
   discount, 17
Stock market, 9
Stock power, 19
Stop order, 26–27

Tax Reform Act of 1986, 35
Taxes and tax law, 9, 20, 35–37
Timing, 13–14
Trade date, 18
Trading, 18–19
Trading desk or trading post, 25
Treasury bill, 14, 42

Uniform Gifts to Minors Act, 20

JEFFREY B. LITTLE, a finance graduate of New York University, began his Wall Street career in the early 1960s. He has worked as an accountant for a retail brokerage firm, as an instructor of technical analysis in a broker training center, as a securities analyst of technology stocks, and as a portfolio manager and advisory committee member for a major mutual fund. He is a Fellow of the Financial Analysts Federation, a member of the New York Society of Security Analysts, and was formerly a vice-president of an investment counsel firm in Baltimore.

PAUL A. SAMUELSON, senior editorial consultant, is Institute Professor Emeritus at the Massachusetts Institute of Technology. He is author (now coauthor) of the best-selling textbook *Economics*. He served as an adviser to President John F. Kennedy and in 1970 was the first American to win the Nobel Prize in economics.

SHAWN PATRICK BURKE, consulting editor, is a securities analyst with Standard & Poor's Corporation. He has been an internal consultant in industry as well as for a Wall Street investment firm, and he has extensive experience in computer-generated financial modeling and analysis.

ROBERT W. WRUBEL, contributing editor, is an associate editor with *Financial World* magazine and was previously associate financial editor with Boardroom Reports, Inc. A graduate of Yale University, he has been a financial analyst for a Wall Street securities firm and has written extensively on finance and investment topics.

PICTURE CREDITS Arlene Collins/Monkmeyer Press Photo Service: pp. 20, 21; courtesy of F. W. Woolworth Co.: p. 14; Mark Ferri: pp. 39, 40; illustrations by David Garner: pp. 10, 11, 18, 26, 28, 30–31 (graph), 37, 43; Geoge Haling: cover; Christopher Morrow/Stock, Boston: p. 24; Joseph Nettis/Photo Researchers, Inc.: p. 32; Stock, Boston: p. 15; UPI/Bettmann Newsphotos: pp. 8, 35, 36.